THE LAUGH-OUT-LOUD CATS SELL OUT

THE LAUGH-OUT-LOUD CATS SELL OUT

by A. KoFord

Consisting of well over twelve dozen cartoon depictions of the hobo-cat duo Kitteh and Pip. Their escapades, perambulations, and assorted minor crimes are presented as both a diversion and a warning against taking up the yoke of a wandering life.

MAY THE READER BEWARE.

Abrams ComicArts, New York

Editors: Eric Klopfer and Aiah Wieder
Designer: Kara Strubel
Production Manager: Jacqueline Poirier

Library of Congress Control Number: 2008934535

ISBN: 978-0-8109-9571-0

Printed and bound in China
10 9 8 7 6 5 4 3 2 1

Abrams ComicArts books are available at special discounts
when purchased in quantity for premiums and promotions
as well as fundraising or educational use. Special editions
can also be created to specification. For details, contact
specialmarkets@hnabooks.com or the address below.

HNA ▌▌▐▐▐
harry n. abrams, inc.
a subsidiary of La Martinière Groupe

115 West 18th Street
New York, NY 10011
www.hnabooks.com

INTRODUCTION

· · ·

BY JOHN HODGMAN

Good evening.

My name is John Hodgman, and I regret to inform you that the book you hold in your hand is not real.

Do not be alarmed. I am not suggesting that this book is a figment of your imagination. That would suggest that these very words of introduction themselves are a product of your diseased mind. But the fact is that you are not insane, and I do not live inside your head (yet).

No. Obviously this book EXISTS. But as a former professional literary agent, I have had some experience in elaborate literary hoaxes (I'm looking at you, "Michael Chabon"—*ALL of you*). And as a current famous minor television personality, I am naturally a first-class authority on being a fraud.

And so, having carefully examined these *Laugh-Out-Loud Cats* cartoons, I have determined that while they are VERY ENJOYABLE and certainly ABOUT CATS, they were not drawn in 1912, as is claimed.

How can I tell? Three things.

First, the slang used by the cats "Kitteh" and "Pip" is quite contemporary, and almost surely inspired by the "LOLcats," (even the names are similar). If you are not familiar with it, the LOLcat is a popular Internet trend that involves taking pictures of actual live cats at the precise moment they are talking. It's a challenging hobby, requiring considerable skill and patience, and also a computer. It is much, much harder than just sitting down and drawing an old-timey picture of cats.

Second, Kitteh and Pip, you will notice, are portrayed as loveable hoboes. Throughout the strips, they gently chase their small, typically feline desires (naps, stew, and a good game of cards) along the back alleys and meandering country roads of a cartoon version of the early twentieth century.

Now, anyone can tell you that there certainly *were* hobo-cats during this time, but they were vicious creatures who lived cruel lives, and frequently killed their masters.

More telling, however, is the fact that cats did not actually start standing on their hind legs until 1972, after the experiments. And it was not until 1980 that Pip's arbitrary, overwhelming obsession with falling leaves was first bred in the American Shorthair at the Yale Feline Studies lab.

Third, I applied the ACID TEST, which is something of a misnomer, as the test involves no acid at all. Instead, the original, hand-drawn cartoons are simply inserted into a small fire. Based on the burn rate of the paper (Fast! Fast! So merry and fast!), I can attest that those cartoons that survived the process and are now collected here almost certainly were not created before the year 2007.

YES: 2007.

But, you protest, we all remember Aloysius Gamaliel Koford. He was a major historical figure: a daring walrus hunter, statesman, and spy! Why, if it were not for the many folktales and young adult novels based on his life, the whole public image of the cartoonist as a glamorous, sexually confident man of adventure probably would not exist!

But it is so. For my research leads to one inescapable conclusion: Aloysius Koford is nothing but a myth, an Internet rumor, a shadow puppet cast upon the wall, all formed by the twisted, stubby fingers of a man standing in the darkness. A man named ADAM KOFORD.

You continue to protest: ADAM "APE LAD" KOFORD?!? The supposed great-grandson of the now thoroughly debunked Aloysius Koford? But that man is a DISGUSTING NOBODY. How could he possibly be a CARTOONIST?

Let me tell you the story as best as I can reconstruct it.

I first came to know Koford's work some three years ago. I had released a book of fake history entitled *The Areas of My Expertise*. Like all decent reference books, it contained within it a number of handy hobo nicknames—700, to be exact. And soon a friendly Web site would suggest that cartoonists begin illustrating each of the hoboes alluded to in my book and posting them on the site. I trust you see the sense behind all of this, and no further explanation is required.

Now it would seem that this Adam Koford is something of an "Internet user." For, from the beginning of what would be known as the "700 hoboes" project, the "Ape Lad" was among the fastest and most prolific contributors. He drew hoboes in every medium: chalk hoboes and watercolor hoboes; hoboes as they might have been drawn by George Herriman, and hoboes as they might have been drawn by Disney and Al Hirschfeld; and hoboes as they might have been drawn by a young man in Florida with a seemingly bottomless barrel of talent and spare time. He drew all seven hundred, and a hundred more, and then he started all over again.

Intrigued, I did a simple Google search for the term "Ape Lad" (for I am the world's greatest detective), and I found not only Adam Koford, but as well a vertiginous portfolio of non-hobo material, comics and spot illustrations in every historical style, each one singing with the Ape Lad's intelligence, skill, and good humor.

Soon I would see his name everywhere on the Internet, and then in *The New Yorker*. And then finally, *The Laugh-Out-Loud Cats* debuted, his signature achievement. For those of us who had followed his work, it seemed at once a perfect tweaking of the Internet that he makes his home, filtered through his own encyclopedic nostalgia for the comics form and the hobo obsessive disorder/general mania (HOD/GMan) that is his sad affliction.

And since he just can't stop creating, Koford then created a creator—Aloysius Koford—as though discovering a secret pile of cartoons was the only way to explain his incredible daily output. As though the ruse and the joke would apologize and distract us from the fact that he had created something better than the Internet memes that had inspired it.

For more than that, so much more, *The Laugh-Out-Loud Cats* is a thing of intrinsic smarts and beauty. It is always clever in its wordplay ("Cognito," announces Pip in a ridiculous false beard, "We are in it"). But glib, it is un-it. Rather, in its sincerity and unfussy, beautiful craftsmanship, it rivals the best of the old-fashioned strips it seeks to emulate. And yes, I am including *Krazy Kat* in that group, because that has only one cat in it, and this one has two.

Since then, I have had the chance to meet Adam Koford. We had dinner and drinks, and I can tell you that he is not a walrus hunter. He is a normal person with a wife and three children. At dinner he eats moderately, and at drinks he does not drink, but he is still good, sweet company. He is not a madman or a spy or an eccentric. He is simply a genius. And that, frankly, is far more exciting, and surprising.

I hope and trust you will enjoy this work, as fraudulent as it is. Now I must go and set to work proving that *Get Fuzzy* is actually written by Thomas Pynchon.

That is all.

JOHN HODGMAN is the author of *The Areas of My Expertise* and *More Information Than You Require*, and a contributor to *The Daily Show* and *The New York Times Magazine*. He lives in New York City.

PLEASE NOTE:

Depending on whom you choose to believe, the comics contained in this volume supposedly appeared in newspapers from 1912 to 1914. They may or may not have been created by one Aloysius Gamaliel Koford: walrus hunter, spy, hobo, mountain man, retired U.S. senator, and cartoonist.

At the time of publication, Aloysius was unable to be reached for comment. According to his great-grandson Adam Koford (the curator and probable creator of this volume), Aloysius, now one hundred and seventeen years old, is currently manning a numbers station on Pitcairn Island and not at all interested in discussing his career as a cartoonist. For this we apologize.

This volume may be an exact replica of a previously unknown 1967 collection of Aloysius's work. Every effort has been made to preserve its value as a cultural artifact and possible hoax.

21

29

45

48

70

133

The comic presented above was found in the archives and, even after extensive restoration efforts, remains impossible to decipher.

A FINAL NOTE

from Aloysius Koford:

4 . . . 26 . . . 27 . . . 3 . . . 52 . . . 3

• SPECIAL THANX •

MELVIN
DIANE

XENI, MARK, CORY, DAVID & ALL TEH HAPPY MUTANTS

HOBOES EVRYWHERE

GEORGE, HANK, WALT & SPARKY

ALEX SANTOSO

TEH FOUNDLINGS & EACH & EVRY OWNR OF AN ORIGINAL COMIC.

• ERIC KLOPFER
• AIAH WIEDER
• LESLIE STOKER
• JACQUIE POIRIER
• MICHAEL JACOBS
• MAXINE KAPLAN
• MICHELLE ISHAY

• & JOHN HODGMAN